Seeing His Heart in Yours

40 Intimate Moments with God

Kathy Proctor

Inks and Bindings
888-290-5218
www.inksandbindings.com
orders@inksandbindings.com

Contents

Dedication

To my husband, Bryan

To my children, Shelby, Shannon and Blake, their spouses, Dane, Nathan and Natalie.

To my grandchildren, Paisley, Haven, Lainey, Samuel, Norah, Leilani and Eli.

From my heart to yours, I love you all dearly, your presence in my life has been an incredible blessing from the Lord. Thank you for your love, support and prayers.

Foreword

There are many things in our daily lives that we want to stay fresh: a heavenly loaf of bread, a juicy red strawberry, a fresh cup of coffee in the morning, and slipping into bed with freshly laundered sheets at night. And best of all is being able to take a big breath of fresh air!

There is also something else that gives us endless possibilities: a fresh perspective where we find new understanding of the divine.

In this second edition of *See His Heart in Yours*, my friend, Kathy Proctor has given us an innovative look at her devotional with new illustrations from her personal walk with Christ.

In this book she grapples with the same issues that stymie our ability to function well. She has lived through the grief we have experienced that relinquishes every feeling, every movement, every breath groping for relief and a glimmer of hope.

She recognizes the kind of anxiety that bleeds through our veins, freezing our concentration and interrupting rational thought.

She understands the plight of mothers in distress, children in need, and caregivers who have given up caring for themselves.

But she also knows the joy and love created by a life lived for her Heavenly Father.

Kathy has explored the Scriptures daily and found nuggets of wisdom and a wealth of understanding from the endless love story between us and our beautiful Savior.

Scripture is the living and breathing Word of God. Kathy knows it well and, in this book, has given us a place to write and pray and find the fresh perspective that is our personal application from what we read.

I know Kathy; she has already prayed for you to be blessed by God in this 40-day journey. It will be refreshment for my soul as I know it will be for you!

Sherri Maxson

Preface

Dearest Reader,

First and foremost, thank you for choosing this book to read in your quiet time. We all face busy lives. Our time is divided between family, job, school, church and many other commitments.

Inspite of the busyness, it's important for us to spend time with the Lord. My hope for you is that you will be able to set aside time in your day for prayer and reflection. May this time spent with the Lord inspire and encourage you.

Wherever the Lord has you right now, may His word and my shared thoughts help you along this life journey our Lord has graciously placed you on. This is from my grateful heart to yours, with love and prayers.

Kathy Proctor

Introduction

Beloved Reader,

As you go through this forty day devotional journal, I urge you to pay close attention to the Bible verse that begins each devotion. Read the verse, meditate on it and look it up in your own Bible. Then go over the short reading for the day. Consider how the verse applies to that days reading and how the verse with the reading applies to your own life. Repeat the prayer at the end of the days reading. Use the journal pages to write out your own prayers and reflection. As you read, pray and reflect, may you realize how much richer knowing the Lord makes each day.

Firmly Planted

He will be like a tree firmly planted by streams of water, which yields its fruit in its season and its leaf does not wither; and in whatever he does he prospers.

—Psalm 1:3 (NASB)

If you have ever observed the sunflower in a field or meadow you would have noticed that the bloom of the sunflower will face the east in the morning and follow the sun all day long. It will actually seek out and face the sun. What you may not know is that their roots grow deep, they can stand tall in a storm and they can stand a dry spell because of how deep their roots spread underground.

When we apply this to our own walk with the Lord it could cause us to think about our loyalty, our adoration and our faith. When it comes to our faith and standing firm we have a genuine responsibility to plant our roots deep into His word and be confident in what it teaches. Faith is about being sure and certain of something. We can stand firm on the truth of His word because we know that God is faithful in His promises and He will always be true to His word. When a storm comes into our life we can stand tall and endure it because our roots are planted deep. Our faith and trust goes beyond what we can see and rests in what we know about our Heavenly Father. In all circumstances we will seek His face and follow Him morning until night. Our loyalty will be with God alone and our adoration is for the one True God.

The sunflower is a beautiful part of God's creation and serves as a reminder to us to always seek the face of the "Son", to plant our roots deep and to stand tall and confident in the storms of life. Are the roots of your faith planted deep? Where does your loyalty lie? What or who has the priority of your adoration?

PRAYER:

Heavenly Father, thank you for the beautiful sunflowers. They help to remind us of your love and faithfulness but also they remind us to follow You in all circumstances. May we plant our roots deep in You and Your word. Amen.

Journal Page
Use this page for reflection, write down your thoughts and prayers

JOURNAL PAGE
Use this page for reflection, write down your thoughts and prayers

God Our Comforter

Blessed be the God and Father of our Lord Jesus Christ, the Father of mercies and God of all comfort, who comforts us in all our affliction so that we will be able to comfort those who are in any affliction with the comfort with which we ourselves are comforted by God.

—2. Corinthians 1:3-4 (NASB)

We may feel at times that life is like one very long winter. Our days feel bitter, cold and barren. Loneliness and grief may overwhelm us. Sorrow could be filling our hearts and minds. I faced such a time in my own life after the death of my dad. I was blessed to have had a close relationship with my dad. As I grieved his death I struggled with life without him in it. Reality was sinking in that I would never hear his voice, see his smile or feel his rough, strong hands in mine. There was just so much to miss, how would I carry on? As the days, weeks and months went on the waves of grief didn't overwhelm me as they had right after his death. Turning to my Lord daily brought the comfort I needed. I found that nothing compares to His comfort in difficult times. I also experienced the comfort of family and friends who also had been through the loss of a loved one. I'm thankful for how the Lord provides in times of need. Life without my dad has been different and difficult at times, but I have carried on with the help of the Lord and loved ones. The comfort of the Lord is like the sunshine that peaks through in the spring after a very long, cold winter. It brings hope that we are going to be okay, that the winter is ending and spring is rushing in. This is the hope the Lord provides when He sustains and strengthens us during our times of grief and sorrow

The word comfort in the above verse means to come alongside to help. The Lord comes alongside us in our time of need so we can come alongside someone else in their time of need. We experience the Lord's love when He comforts us, and we share the Lord's love when we comfort others. Nothing can prevent the suffering that comes with living our life but nothing compares to the comfort the Lord gives to His children.

Do you need God's comfort today? Do you need to be the comfort for someone facing affliction?

PRAYER:

Thank you, Lord, for extending Your comfort and peace in the midst of heartache. Thank you for the strength to endure during times of affliction. May we be sensitive to the opportunities to help others in their time of affliction. Amen.

Journal Page
Use this page for reflection, write down your thoughts and prayers

Journal Page

Use this page for reflection, write down your thoughts and prayers

The Master's Chisel

For we are His workmanship (masterpiece) created in Christ Jesus for good works, which God prepared beforehand, that we should walk in them.

—Ephesians 2:10 (NASB)

What comes to mind when you think of an artist's masterpiece? Is it the artist or the work of art? The work of such famous artists as DiVinci, Michelangelo, Van Gogh, and Picasso could cause us to think of their body of work, but also their mastery in the work. These legends of art showed devotion, dedication, and authority in carrying out their finished masterpieces.

When Michelangelo sculpted the statue of David, he had to devote time, sacrifice, and precision to accomplish such a magnificent masterpiece. From one very large piece of marble, he had to envision the finished work. He had to know exactly where to strike the blow of his chisel. With each strike of the chisel, whether small or large, it had to be precise. Each strike caused another piece of marble to fall, and with each strike, another part of his masterpiece was revealed. He struck the hammer and chisel to cut away any unnecessary marble until the beauty of his masterpiece was finished. If you have ever viewed the statue of David, it is awe-inspiring, just magnificent!

As the verse above states, we are God's workmanship, His masterpiece, but to become His finished work, He may have to use His chisel in our lives. It may be necessary for Him to cut away things in our lives like a bad attitude, an unhealthy relationship, or a habit that has taken up too much time. Some blows of the chisel are more painful than others, but are necessary in order to ultimately become who He wants us to be. Remember that God is devoted, dedicated, and has the authority to do what He sees as necessary to produce His masterpiece. He sees the final product. He uses His sovereign chisel to cut away everything that doesn't fit the masterpiece that He is creating.

What in your life needs to be cut away? Are you willing to surrender to the Master's chisel?

PRAYER:

Lord, may we surrender to the cutting away of unnecessary things in our lives, unhealthy things, and anything that will keep us from becoming who you desire us to be. We realize that you see the finished product. Thank you for loving us so completely. Amen.

Journal Page
Use this page for reflection, write down your thoughts and prayers

JOURNAL PAGE
Use this page for reflection, write down your thoughts and prayers

God Cares for Us

Casting all your anxiety on Him, because He cares for you.
—1Peter 5:7 (NASB)

Casting means to throw something onto something else. As Christians, we are to cast all of our discontent, discouragement, and despair on the Lord and trust Him for what He is doing in our lives. It's easy to say but hard to do. I'm the worst at releasing my anxiety, worry, or stress upon the Lord. Instead, I hold onto it and fret over it to the point of losing sleep at night. When I finally surrender my control over a situation and trust the Lord to take care of it, peace enters my heart and mind. It's foolish of me to hold onto my anxiety when I know that the Lord is more than capable of handling the problem that has entered my life. The Lord has proven that He is trustworthy and faithful in my life, so I just need to surrender. Let me encourage the person who may struggle to cast their worry, stress, or anxiety upon the Lord, when you finally cast it all on His very capable shoulders, you will feel relief. Remember that when things become difficult for us, there is nothing too hard for the Lord. Believing and resting in that truth will protect your mind, heart, and spirit from the overload of stress. We can also be confident that He cares for us. If He didn't, would He have sent Jesus into the world to die for us? Of course not! That is why we can always turn to Him for the help we need.

What cares and anxieties do you need to bring to the Lord?

PRAYER:

Lord, help us in our time of need. Life can overwhelm us at times, please remind us of Your care for us. May we cast our cares, one by one, upon Your capable shoulders. Thank you for your faithfulness and unconditional love. Amen.

Journal Page
Use this page for reflection, write down your thoughts and prayers

JOURNAL PAGE
Use this page for reflection, write down your thoughts and prayers

Inner Peace

Be anxious for nothing, but in everything by prayer and supplication with thanksgiving let your requests be known to God. And the peace of God, which surpasses all understanding, will guard your hearts and minds in Christ Jesus.

—Philippians 4:6-7 (NASB)

Inner peace can be defined as an inner calm or tranquility. This type of peace is promised to the Christian who has a thankful attitude based on an unwavering confidence that God is able and willing to do what is best for His children. Peace is more than a mere word, idea, or feeling. It is actually a gift of God to those who choose to walk by faith in Jesus Christ. This gift of peace can be achieved when our lives are in the right place with the Lord. When we submit our anxiety, our worries, our insecurities, our doubts, and all areas of our lives to Him in prayer, we will experience this peace that the Bible talks about. As the verse above states, it's a peace beyond our understanding, and this peace will guard our hearts from anxiety, doubt, and fear. When we offer a trusting heart to God we can count on peace to enter in.

Are you searching for peace apart from Christ? Surrender all to Him, and you will experience His peace.

PRAYER:

Lord, it is through us giving all to you that we will experience Your gift of inner peace. Please take away our anxious thoughts, our doubts, and our fears, and replace them with Your peace. Thank you for the gift of peace. Amen.

Journal Page
Use this page for reflection, write down your thoughts and prayers

JOURNAL PAGE
Use this page for reflection, write down your thoughts and prayers

Where Does Your Treasure Lie?

Don't store up treasure here on earth, where moths eat them
and rust destroys them and where thieves break in and steal.
Store your treasures in heaven, where moths and rust can
not destroy, and thieves do not break in and steal. Wherever
your treasure is, there the desires of your heart will also be.

—Matthew 6:19-21 (NLT)

We have a tendency to place security in material things. Jesus is telling us that any type of material treasure on earth can either be destroyed by elements of nature (moths and rust) or stolen by thieves. Jesus says that the only investments not subject to loss are treasures in heaven. The Lord takes an interest in how we use our finances, our time and our talents. Let's say if we owned real estate, we would follow the housing market with genuine interest. If we had financial investments, we would follow the stock market closely. If we had treasure in heaven, guess where our interest would lie? Our interest would be with Jesus in heaven.

Our material possessions are temporary and have no eternal value. It doesn't mean we shouldn't have any earthly possessions, it's the value and importance we place on them that matters. Jesus wants our hearts and anything that comes between His possession of our heart should not have a place in our lives.

When we use our finances to further the spread of the gospel; when we use our time in ministry; when we use our talents to glorify the Lord; these all make deposits into our treasury in heaven, for all eternity. When Jesus is the top priority in our life, our treasure will be in heaven and our earthly possessions will have less of a priority in our lives.

Does your treasure lie in earthly possessions or in the things that have eternal value?

PRAYER:

Lord, we pray that we would use our finances, our time, and our talents to glorify You. May we place more importance on those things that have eternal value? May it be evident where our true treasure lies, with You in heaven. Amen.

JOURNAL PAGE
Use this page for reflection, write down your thoughts and prayers

Journal Page
Use this page for reflection, write down your thoughts and prayers

The Narrow And Wide Gates

Enter through the narrow gate; for the gate is wide and the way is broad that leads to destruction, and there are many who enter through it. For the gate is small and the way narrow that leads to life, and there are few who find it.

—Matthew 7:13-14 (NASB)

We have the freedom to make choices in life, and our choices have consequences. The above verses serve as a warning to us. We have a choice to make, and we need to choose wisely.

Through the narrow gate, life is more difficult. It will require us to repent of our sins, to exhibit discipline in our lives, to obey God's word and to walk by faith. We will face trials and tribulations, but Jesus will guide us through and refine us. Ultimately, the narrow gate leads us to life eternal with our Savior, Jesus Christ. Choosing the wide gate will be an easier, more comfortable life. It will be a life of self-indulgence and pleasure, you will have more company because more choose this gate, but it will lead to destruction. Life through the wide gate may seem more appealing, but it will ultimately cause us to be separated from the Lord for all eternity.

The difficult life through the narrow gate is the only life worth living, the consequence is eternal life with Jesus. The easy life through the wide gate will bring temporary pleasure; the consequence is eternal separation from Jesus.

Which gate will you choose, the narrow or the wide?

PRAYER:

Lord, thank you for making a way for us through the narrow gate. We know that narrow is the way that leads to life. It comforts us to know that You are with us every step of the way. Amen.

JOURNAL PAGE
Use this page for reflection, write down your thoughts and prayers

JOURNAL PAGE

Use this page for reflection, write down your thoughts and prayers

Beauty Through God's Eyes

Beauty can be defined in many ways, our world has distorted the definition. Our world places too much worth on the outside appearance. Beauty is more than skin deep—it starts in the heart and works outward. God's beautiful woman is: pure, honest, thrifty, kind, wise and holy. These internal qualities enable her to manage her life, her time, her money, her relationships, and herself.

Let's look a little deeper into the verse above. I also encourage you to read all of Proverbs 31, it gives a more complete picture of God's beautiful woman. As the verse states, charm is deceitful. Charm is fleeting. Charm is fickle. Charm can lure and fascinate, but it is short-lived. It is not a quality that deepens into our hearts and produces beauty from within.

And it also states that beauty is vain. This is outward beauty, which is only skin deep. Although everyone appreciates loveliness of form, physical beauty is temporary. Beauty by appearance alone is fleeting, fading and nothing but a vapor. The beauty that we are striving for is one that begins in the heart and overflows outward, a lasting beauty. In order to have the inward beauty that God desires, we have to work on being a woman of noble character.

As we see at the end of the verse, the woman who fears the Lord shall be praised. God's beautiful woman is a woman who loves

Him and has reverence for Him. Let this woman be honored for her diligence and noble character.

We are to seek the praise of God rather than men. We are to shun the transitory vanities of this world and pursue instead the eternal beauty of the Lord. This is no easy task. When we commit to spend time with the Lord in prayer and Bible reading, this will help to ground us and develop internal qualities that honor God.

How can you nurture your commitment to the Lord? What do you have to do to develop the inward qualities that will make you God's beautiful woman?

PRAYER:

Lord, it is our desire to focus more on our inward beauty. Help us to work on those qualities that will grow us from the inside to flow outward. May we be women of noble character and may our lives glorify You. Amen.

JOURNAL PAGE
Use this page for reflection, write down your thoughts and prayers

JOURNAL PAGE
Use this page for reflection, write down your thoughts and prayers

Legacy

Tell your sons about it, and let your sons tell their sons, and
their sons the next generation.

—Joel 1:3 (NASB)

Legacy can have a few definitions: it can be an inheritance left by a loved one, it can be a characteristic derived from our ancestors, or it can be a way of life—our conduct that is remembered after someone passes away. The latter is the definition that I am focusing on here. Every day, each one of us is adding something to the portrait of our lives. Whether good or bad, our decisions, our priorities, and our habits will remain at least for a time, for others to reflect upon and consider. We are all leaving a legacy. It should way heavy on our minds and hearts the responsibility we hold as parents and grandparents, the type of legacy we will leave for our loved ones. Will it be a legacy of faithfulness, humility, integrity—one that points to Christ? This type of legacy will be remembered with affection. Will it be a legacy of pride, distraction, impatience, one that points to self? This type of legacy will be remembered with resentment.

As Christians, our desire should be to leave a legacy that honors the Lord and reflects His love. We should share with our children and grandchildren the mighty acts of faithfulness that the Lord performed in our lives, how He protected, provided, and comforted. We share this testimony so future generations can share it with their children.

I have been blessed to have married into a Christian family. Those who have passed, like my mother-in-law and my husband's grandmother, left behind a rich legacy of their Christian faith. They both modeled a life of humility, devotion, and service. It serves as a reminder for us, their family, on how to live out our Christian lives.

There is no greater heritage you can leave your family than the memory of a loved one who faithfully served the Lord.

What type of legacy are you leaving for your family?

Prayer:

Heavenly Father, thank you for the gift of those who have left our generation a rich spiritual heritage. Help us to be just as faithful and to point our loved ones to You. May we leave a legacy of faith that will be remembered for generations. Amen.

Journal Page
Use this page for reflection, write down your thoughts and prayers

JOURNAL PAGE
Use this page for reflection, write down your thoughts and prayers

Kindness

Let the love of the brethren continue. 2 Do not neglect to show hospitality to strangers, for by this some have entertained angels without knowing it.

—Hebrews 13:1-2 (NASB)

When we are on the receiving end of an act of kindness from a friend, family member, or even stranger, it encourages us, lifts our spirits, and blesses us. When we are the one who extends the act of kindness, it also blesses us. To be able to extend a helping hand or extend some encouragement to someone brings joy and blessing to our hearts. The far-reaching effect of an act of kindness can be compared to throwing a rock in a lake, and the rings of the water ripple out.

One ripple leads to the next and the next, before you know it there are multiple rings connected to the first ripple. So it is when we extend love and kindness to one another. One act of kindness leads to another and so on. One never knows how far-reaching an act of kindness might be. Let's keep our eyes open for opportunities to extend God's love, kindness, and compassion. Who knows we may be entertaining angels without knowing it!

Who needs to know they are loved today? Who can you show hospitality to?

PRAYER:

Lord, may we be quick to lend a helping hand. Help us, Lord, to put ourselves aside and think of the needs of those around us. We thank you for giving us these opportunities to extend love and kindness. Amen.

Journal Page
Use this page for reflection, write down your thoughts and prayers

JOURNAL PAGE
Use this page for reflection, write down your thoughts and prayers

He Is With You Always

Be strong and courageous, do not be afraid or tremble at them, for the Lord your God is the one who goes with you. He will not fail you or forsake you.

—Deuteronomy 31:6 (NASB)

Our strength and courage to live out these precious days the Lord has given us should come with the confidence of knowing the Lord will not leave us or forsake us. Wherever we are and whatever we face He is with us. This life can bring uncertainty and sorrow but also pleasure and happiness. In all circumstances, good or bad we can be sure we are not alone. The Lord shares all of our days with us.

When my son was just a baby he had to have a heart scan because of a possible heart condition.

It was an uncertain time but I was reminded by a precious sister in Christ that God was always with me and my baby. This reminder helped as my son was put under anesthesia and as we waited for results. Whatever the outcome God would not fail or forsake us. Thankfully the results were good, no surgery was required.

This promise reassures us there is absolutely no way whatsoever that God will EVER leave us.

You need never to fear God has not forgotten you.

Are you facing an uncertain time? God is with you always and will not forsake you!

PRAYER:

Thank you Lord for the promise that You will never leave or forsake us. We are assured to never be alone, You are always by our side. Amen.

Journal Page
Use this page for reflection, write down your thoughts and prayers

JOURNAL PAGE
Use this page for reflection, write down your thoughts and prayers

Ready to Forgive

For Thou art good, and ready to forgive, and abundant in
loving kindness to all who call upon Thee.

—Psalm 86:5 (NASB)

When I was a little girl, I took a piece of bubble gum from a local general store. I was with my mom, and she noticed that I took the piece of gum without paying for it. She told me that I had to go back into the store and give the gum back to the man behind the counter. I hated the thought of admitting my guilt to that man. We couldn't go home until I did. So, I went back into the store.

I gave the man back the gum, admitted my guilt, and apologized. He was very kind and gracious. He could tell that my apology was sincere. He accepted my apology —he forgave me. I continued to go to the store from time to time; he never mentioned the gum incident to me again. It was just like it hadn't happened.

When we fall short and commit a sin, our Heavenly Father doesn't overlook the sin but is ready to forgive it if we confess it to Him. Be assured that you have been forgiven, and He has forgotten about that sin. In Micah 7:19, it states, "You will tread our sins underfoot and hurl all our iniquities into the depths of the sea." What a comfort it is to know we are forgiven and our sins forgotten, not to be brought up again!

Is there someone in your life that you need to extend forgiveness to, just as that store clerk forgave me? Is there sin in your life that needs to be confessed? Don't delay, do it today!

PRAYER:

Lord, thank you for the gift of forgiveness. May we have the courage to forgive others who have wronged us. May we also have the courage to confess our sins to You, knowing that they will be forgiven and forgotten. Amen.

Journal Page
Use this page for reflection, write down your thoughts and prayers

Journal Page
Use this page for reflection, write down your thoughts and prayers

God As Our Refuge

The Lord is my rock and my fortress and my deliverer. My God, my rock, in whom I take refuge; my shield and the horn of my salvation, my stronghold and my refuge; my savior, You save me from violence.

—2 Samuel 22:2-3 (NASB)

These verses are a song of praise and thanksgiving from the heart of David as he describes God's deliverance from his enemies. He describes Him as his rock, fortress, refuge, and shield. These are places of security and safety, a place out of harm's way. When trouble or temptation threatens to overwhelm us, we can turn to God as our safe haven. We all need a safe place where we know that we are protected and loved. When we run to Him, He welcomes us, He defends our honor, and He preserves our lives. A fortress is a building that the enemy cannot penetrate. The Lord is a mighty fortress for His own, where they can find refuge and security.

When I was a little girl, I loved to build forts out of blankets, sheets, and folding chairs. My own little place of refuge. There was just something about reading a book or playing with my dolls in my own little space that made me feel safe and secure. What a great feeling that was at the time. The Lord can be that place for us as we face uncertainty in our lives. Ask Him to shelter you with His unconditional, unfailing love. We can be certain that when we turn to Him in troubled times, He is there for us. Psalm 46:1 states, "God is our refuge and strength. A very present help in trouble." God is our defense, refuge, and deliverer.

Are you facing uncertain times right now? Do you need the shelter of His protection? Don't delay, turn to Him today.

PRAYER:

Lord, we come to You with thanksgiving in our hearts because of how You have been our refuge, strength, and protection. Please continue to shelter us with Your unconditional love. Amen.

JOURNAL PAGE
Use this page for reflection, write down your thoughts and prayers

JOURNAL PAGE
Use this page for reflection, write down your thoughts and prayers

Miracles

How great are His signs, how powerful His wonders! His kingdom will last forever, His rule through all generations.
—Daniel 4:3 (NLT)

During my childhood, I was sure to attend the county fair whenever it was in town. One of the exhibits I enjoyed was the miniature train exhibit. It was like looking into a miniature wonderland. There were neighborhoods with people in the streets, shopping centers, mountains, lakes, highways, and bridges. Several trains would make their way through this miniature town. When something needed to be changed or repaired, there was a gentleman who would take care of it. If a train derailed, a building fell over, or a mountain needed to be moved, he would walk into this "little world" and create a miracle. He would fix the derailment, put the building back in place, and move the mountain. You get the picture! He would come in with his big, strong hands and fix the situation.

This is how our Heavenly Father works in our lives. He comes into the very world that He created, intervenes in the lives of His children, and performs a miracle with ease. Because He is sovereign, He is all-powerful, and because He can! We may not have seen the parting of the Red Sea or the feeding of 5000 people lately, but He heals the cancer patient, He mends broken hearts, and restores broken marriages. These are the miracles of our day. He provides in extraordinary ways for the needs of His children. He reaches down with His big, strong hands and takes care of the situation. He can actually move a mountain if He wanted to. His signs and wonders are all around us. We need to be on the lookout for them and praise Him in the process. One day, a miracle will occur for all to see, the day Jesus returns for His church-be ready!

What miracle is God performing in your life today? Be looking for them and be thankful.

PRAYER:

Lord, we thank you for performing miracles in our lives every day. Help us to be sensitive to see them around us. Thank you, Father, for intervening in our lives with Your power, wisdom, and healing touch. We love you! Amen.

JOURNAL PAGE
Use this page for reflection, write down your thoughts and prayers

Journal Page
Use this page for reflection, write down your thoughts and prayers

Hold on Tight

On a flight home after visiting family in Arkansas (when I still lived in California), the plane I was on started to experience some turbulence. I observed a little girl across the aisle from me. She became scared and reached for her mom's hand. The little girl's mom reached over and took her hand and said," Hold on tight, baby, it will be all right." They held hands for a while, and then the little girl was all right. All she needed was the touch of her mom's hand. This little girl felt comfort and security from her mom being close and holding her hand.

When we face times of uncertainty and adversity, God is there for us. Our Comforter soothes in various ways—through Scripture, through hymns, through our family, friends, and through us reaching out to Him in prayer. These are ways our Heavenly Father holds our hand when we experience difficult times in our lives. We could almost hear Him saying to us," Sweet hurting child, you are special to Me. I hurt with you. I'm staying right here to take care of you.' We can be assured that He will never leave us alone in our adversity.

Will you trust Him today to get you through the turbulence in your life?

PRAYER:

Lord, what a comfort to know You are always there. May we have the courage to rest in You during difficult times. May we also reach out and take comfort in Your hand and hold on tight. It may be a bumpy ride, but we know you'll see us through. Amen.

JOURNAL PAGE
Use this page for reflection, write down your thoughts and prayers

JOURNAL PAGE
Use this page for reflection, write down your thoughts and prayers

Pruning

All discipline for the moment seems not to be joyful,
but sorrowful; yet to those who have been trained by it,
afterwards it yields the peaceful fruit of righteousness.

—Hebrews 12:11(NASB)

My parents were apple farmers during the years of their retirement. They had 200 beautiful apple trees of several varieties. There was a specific time during the year when the trees required pruning. So my husband and I packed up the kids and headed to the farm to help in the pruning process. The pruning was necessary for the health of the trees and so that the trees would produce good fruit during the harvest. What a harvest, too! Some of the best apples around. It would of been foolish and negligent of my parents to ignore what was best for the growth of their trees.

Pruning in the Christians life takes place as well; it usually involves the discomfort of discipline and the removal of areas of our life that keep us from proper growth. When God lovingly tends to those areas in our life like pride, self-sufficiency, and love of self, the qualities that choke out growth, even though it may be painful, it is for our good. As the above verse states, after the discipline, we will yield the fruit of righteousness. What is the fruit of righteousness? It is good works with the right motive, those works that glorify God, not ourselves. It is growth and refinement necessary in the Christians life. It would be unloving for God to leave us to ourselves, even though we may think we know best. God's discipline is perfect and always for the good of His children. Pruning occurs just for a season, but the result is good fruit.

What areas in your life need to be pruned? How is God pruning you for your good?

PRAYER:

Lord, we know that You discipline us because You love us and desire for us to grow. Help us not to resist Your hand of pruning, and may it result in the fruit that brings You glory. Amen.

Journal Page
Use this page for reflection, write down your thoughts and prayers

JOURNAL PAGE
Use this page for reflection, write down your thoughts and prayers

The Reassuring Quality of God's Faithfulness

> Know therefore that the Lord your God, He is God, the faithful God, who keeps His covenant and His lovingkindness to the thousandth generation, with those who love Him and keep His commandments.
> —Deuteronomy 7:9 (NASB)

There are many qualities of God revealed in Scripture, and one of them is His faithfulness. You may ask how God displays His faithfulness. We can see in Scripture that He always does what He has said and fulfills every promise He's made. He never forgets, falters, or fails to keep His word. He is reliable, trustworthy, unfailing, unwavering, constant, and steadfast. This is who God is all the time—in the light or darkness, in good times or bad. His unchanging nature is the essence of His faithfulness.

When I think back over the 50 + years I have been a Christian, I can see God's faithful hand all over my life. He has been faithful to provide for my needs and my family's needs. He has been faithful to comfort in sorrow, faithful to strengthen, faithful to equip in ministry and service, and faithful to hedge my family and me in His protection. God has proven Himself faithful in my life, and I am eternally grateful.

God extends His faithfulness to His children out of His great love for them. Our unfaithfulness does not nullify His faithfulness because it's one of His unchanging attributes. He will extend it to us "to the thousandth generation," which means forever! We are incredibly blessed to be able to rest in the assurance that God will always keep His promises and forever extend His faithfulness to us, His children.

In what ways has God demonstrated His faithfulness in your life?

PRAYER:

Lord, we thank you for your faithfulness in our lives. May we rest in the assurance that no matter the circumstance, You are reliable, trustworthy, unfailing, unwavering, constant, and steadfast. We are eternally grateful. Amen.

Journal Page
Use this page for reflection, write down your thoughts and prayers

Journal Page
Use this page for reflection, write down your thoughts and prayers

Tapestry

And we know that God causes all things to work together
for good to those who love God, to those who are called
according to His purpose.

—Romans 8:28 (NASB)

When I was a little girl, I loved playing with my sewing cards. I would pull different colored thread with a needle through prepunched holes to form a pretty picture on the front of the card. The back of the card was a mess—thread here and there, in no order. If my focus were on the back of the card, I would miss the pretty picture on the front. As in life, if we focus on the negative things that are happening in our lives, we will miss the beautiful picture God is weaving of our lives.

It may not always seem as though God is working all things to work together for good when we are facing heartbreak, loss, disappointment, frustration, or tragedy in our lives. We may wonder, how can good come from all of this? We have to muster up the courage to trust that God has a plan and purpose for the adversity. God, in His sovereignty, takes our joys and sorrows, our bad times and good times, and weaves them together to create a beautiful tapestry of our life. In God's providence, He orchestrates every event in life—do we always understand why? No, we don't, that's where our trust and faith come in. Believing that He is accomplishing a desired outcome in our life. We have to trust Him for the threads that He is weaving in our lives because the finished picture will be a beautiful tapestry. A life filled with courage, obedience, perseverance, love, and faith. What side of the tapestry are you focusing on? Are you focusing on the back with all the messy thread or the front with the beautiful picture?

PRAYER:

Lord, help us not to focus on the negatives in our lives but to place our focus on You and Your plan for us. We know that You are taking ALL situations in our lives to accomplish Your purpose. Thank you for working all things together to form a beautiful tapestry of our life. Amen.

Journal Page
Use this page for reflection, write down your thoughts and prayers

JOURNAL PAGE
Use this page for reflection, write down your thoughts and prayers

Prayer

Confess your sins to each other and pray for each other that you may be healed. The prayer of a righteous person has great power and produces wonderful results.

—James 5:16 (NLT)

Prayer is one of the most important activities in a Christians life because we are actually talking to the sovereign God of the universe who has all power and knowledge. He understands how we feel, knows what we think, and has the power to intervene in every area of life. Like any relationship, it is essential that we spend time with the person we love. Relationships with little to no communication become distant and shallow. To help keep our relationship with the Lord close and have depth, we need to talk with Him. Scripture repeatedly tells us to devote ourselves to prayer (Colossians 4:2). Devotion not only requires us to set aside uninterrupted time for prayer, but also that we think seriously about what we are saying to the Lord.

What a blessing it has been as a mom to have heard my children's prayers when they were young. Their prayers were honest, real, and straightforward. I often think of those prayers and realize my prayers need to be more like theirs. We can't say anything to the Lord that He doesn't already know, so let's not try to hide behind the truth.

Jesus set a perfect example of a healthy prayer life. He was devoted to time in prayer with His Father. He went to Him with thanksgiving, for strength and for comfort. He went to Him morning, noon, and night—alone and in public. His example is one we should follow.

Prayer is a channel through which we build an intimate relationship with God and sense His unconditional love for us.

How can we make prayer a daily lifestyle? What prompts or hinders us from spending time in prayer?

PRAYER:

Heavenly Father, we come before You today and recognize Your sovereignty and Your unconditional love. We thank you for always being there to hear our prayers at any time of day. We come to You with open hearts, help us to face the challenges of this day. Amen.

JOURNAL PAGE
Use this page for reflection, write down your thoughts and prayers

JOURNAL PAGE
Use this page for reflection, write down your thoughts and prayers

Leftovers

> You also say, "My how tiresome it is! And you disdainfully sniff at it," says the Lord of Hosts, and you bring what was taken by robbery and what is lame or sick; so you bring the offering! Should I receive that from your hand? says the Lord.
>
> —Malachi 1:13 (NASB)

Imagine for a moment that you have invited your family over for a holiday dinner. As you prepare for your guests, you place a centerpiece on the table that has been sitting outside in the dirt. The flowers are plastic, weathered, faded, and full of dirt and leaves. Then you begin to prepare the meal, and you proceed to take food from the trashcan that has been thrown away. Half-eaten apples, veggies, molded bread, and old roast beef. As you collect this food, which is basically garbage, you place it on the table to serve to your guests. You get the picture! Placing a weathered centerpiece on the table and serving your loved ones leftover garbage for a meal would be unheard of. Wouldn't you want to offer only the best to your loved ones?

The people of Israel were guilty of offering God their leftovers for a sacrifice. They would use blind, diseased, and crippled animals for their sacrifices. This showed such disrespect to the Lord and profaned the altar of the Almighty God.

Don't we do the same when we give the Lord our second best? When we give Him our leftover time, our leftover abilities, our leftover money, we are saying He is second in our lives. God deserves only the best from us; anything less shows disrespect. Let's be generous to others, but most importantly, be generous to our Heavenly Father. Consider how we have benefited from God's love and generosity to us. When we hold back and do not give God our best, we say to Him that He is not a priority in our lives.

Are you giving God your leftovers? What needs to change in your life in order to give God your best?

PRAYER:

Lord, forgive us when we offer You our leftovers. Our desire is to offer you only the best. Help us to correctly prioritize our time, talents, and treasure. Amen.

JOURNAL PAGE
Use this page for reflection, write down your thoughts and prayers

Journal Page
Use this page for reflection, write down your thoughts and prayers

God's Love Endures Forever

God's love endures forever; His faithfulness continues through all generations.

—Psalm 100:5 (NASB)

Every generation beginning with Adam and Eve to present day have experienced the love of God. It doesn't end with the current generation, God's love will endure for all future generations as well. When we combine the promise of His love and His faithfulness to continue for all generations, it should bring us comfort, peace and hope. As the world carries on and we observe it's depravity, times of bleakness and chaos we can hold on to this promise that God's love will endure.

I am reminded of this verse when I look in the eyes of my children and grandchildren—the next generations to carry on in my family. Knowing that God has a limitless amount of love to bestow upon them and He will continue to be faithful for all generations gives me a sense of peace. We can trust in the goodness of God. We can be assured He will never leave His throne. We can rest is the promise of His love enduring forever and His faithfulness to continue for ALL generations.

How have you witnessed God's love and faithfulness endure in your family, generation after generation?

PRAYER:

Thank you Lord that Your faithfulness endures through all generations. We are thankful that You have a limitless amount of love to bestow upon us. Amen.

JOURNAL PAGE
Use this page for reflection, write down your thoughts and prayers

JOURNAL PAGE
Use this page for reflection, write down your thoughts and prayers

God Plans for Our Future and Our Hope

For I know the plans I have for you, declares the Lord, plans for welfare and not for calamity to give you a future and a hope.

—Jeremiah 29:11 (NASB)

We don't always understand how God works in our lives, but we can always be sure that He has a plan and purpose for what He is doing. God works through people and circumstances to bring about His perfect will for us. The above verse assured the people of Israel that God's intention for them was to bring about blessing in their future. He intends the same for us.

I was adopted as a newborn, and my adoption was never a secret. My adoptive parents were loving and gracious people, and I had a wonderful childhood. It doesn't change the fact that I was adopted and had questions. When I was in my thirties, I found my birthmother, and many of my questions were answered. In finding her and learning about the details surrounding my adoption, I realized how God, in His faithfulness, protected me from what could have been a very unhappy and tragic childhood. I am incredibly grateful and thankful for God's hand on my life. God took a bad situation and turned it into an opportunity to give me a hopeful future. The love of God shows up in our darkest moments as a light of hope.

How have you seen God work through people and circumstances to bring about His plan for your life?

PRAYER:

Lord, nothing compares to your love for us. Thank you for working out your perfect plan for our lives. Your ways are always best. Amen.

JOURNAL PAGE
Use this page for reflection, write down your thoughts and prayers

JOURNAL PAGE
Use this page for reflection, write down your thoughts and prayers

Testimony

Whatever you do in word or deed, do all in the name of the
Lord Jesus, giving thanks through Him to God the Father.
—Colossians 3:17 (NASB)

We have a personal testimony, which is an expression of what God has done and is doing in our lives. We also have a testimony or a witness that we live out every day by how we conduct our lives. We have to act consistently with who God is and with what He wants. There are three essentials to living out a proper testimony that glorifies God. First, our character needs to be solid. A person who emulates humility, sincerity, courage, integrity, love, and grace. Second, our conduct. Our walk needs to be a godly one. Our conduct should match our character. Third, our conversations. Be mindful of what you are saying to those around you. Do your conversations match your character and conduct?

In our everyday living, people need to see Jesus in our actions, in our words, and in all that we do. When we put Jesus in the center of our lives, the result is that our character, our conduct, and our conversations will honor the Lord. Those who observe our livelihood will see a difference in how we live. This could lead to us sharing our personal testimony. Which could lead someone to come to know Jesus as their Lord and Savior. We never know the influence we actually have, but people watch us—waiting to see if our words match our actions. The above verse says that we are to do all in the name of the Lord Jesus. Simply put, our character, conduct, and conversations should glorify the Lord.

What is our life saying to others about who we are and who Jesus is?

PRAYER:

Lord, help us live our lives as a testimony to You. May our character, conduct, and conversations bring You glory and honor. Amen.

Journal Page

Use this page for reflection, write down your thoughts and prayers

JOURNAL PAGE
Use this page for reflection, write down your thoughts and prayers

A Heart To Serve

The Lord doesn't see things the way you see them. People judge by appearance, but the Lord looks at the heart.

—1 Samuel 16:7 (NLT)

Service for the believer requires the right motive from a pure heart. Oftentimes, we serve with the wrong motives. We may serve to gain approval or acceptance from God or the people around us. We may serve out of guilt. We may serve just to get recognition. Service under these circumstances may result in the gratitude of many, and it may benefit those who have been served. However, it may later result in problems for the person serving with the wrong motivation.

When we serve with the right heart and motivation, the service is done in love and humility. When selfish ambition and selfish desires are set aside, we are able to carry out our service to others unselfishly and bring the proper glory to God.

A heart that is in a consistent relationship with God requires consistent time in prayer and reading the Word, this will produce a heart that is ready to serve. God sees the heart that is humble, willing, and faithful.

What is your motivation to serve? What is the condition of your heart?

PRAYER:

Lord, search our hearts. May our hearts be the ones You use for service, to bring You the proper glory. Amen.

Journal Page
Use this page for reflection, write down your thoughts and prayers

JOURNAL PAGE
Use this page for reflection, write down your thoughts and prayers

Fearfully and Wonderfully Made

I will give thanks to You, for I am fearfully and wonderfully made; wonderful are Your works, and my soul knows it very well.

—Psalm 139:14 (NASB)

God's fingerprints are on each one of us. We are God's creation. We are not an accident. We were created with a purpose in mind. Our beautiful Creator used His hands, His touch, to craft us—His crowning jewel of handiwork. God reached all the way from heaven to touch us and make us His own. Each one of us has a unique eye color, hair color, style of nose, curve of lips, and body shape. We were created with intention and, most importantly, love. God is the master craftsman shaping His work of art, and He gave us the breath of life. His touch separates us from all created things. His touch on our lives reminds us that we are loved and cherished by the Creator of the world.

Praise the Lord today for the wonder of who you are in Christ. Thank Him because in His eyes, you have beauty, worth, and purpose. Can you see His fingerprints on your life?

PRAYER:

Thank you, Lord, for your loving touch on our lives. Keep molding us into the beautiful person You desire us to be. Thank you for loving us so completely.

JOURNAL PAGE
Use this page for reflection, write down your thoughts and prayers

JOURNAL PAGE
Use this page for reflection, write down your thoughts and prayers

A Sure Foundation

He is like a man building a house, who dug deep and laid a foundation on the rock; and when a flood occurred, the torrent burst against the house and could not shake it, because it had been well built.

—Luke 6:48 (NASB)

As I drive to church on Sunday mornings, I drive by an old barn that has weathered many storms. It's leaning to one side but still standing. It must have a solid foundation to still be standing after all of these years and multiple storms.

As Christians it's important for us to have a sure foundation in the Lord so that when trials enter our lives we will not be shaken or crumble. The Christian who has a sure foundation is the one who follows principles of Christian discipleship. These include, praying regularly, reading the Bible, obeying His word and placing your trust in the Lord. This is the right way to build a life with a solid foundation. The wise man builds his house on the Rock, who is Christ; the foolish man builds his house on the sand, he is the one who hears but fails to follow the truth. The foolish man builds his life on what he thinks best, following the carnal principles of this world. When the storms of life rage, his house, which is without foundation is swept away.

How strong is your foundation? Will you collapse when storm hits or will you be able to stand firm?

> **PRAYER:**
>
> Lord, help us to be like the wise man and build our lives in You. May we stay devoted to prayer and Bible reading. We want our lives to be founded on the Rock, Jesus Christ; not founded on the things of this world. Amen.

Journal Page
Use this page for reflection, write down your thoughts and prayers

JOURNAL PAGE
Use this page for reflection, write down your thoughts and prayers

Umbrella of Protection

God is our refuge and strength, a very present help in trouble.
—Psalm 46:1 (NASB)

When we go out in a storm, we will usually bring an umbrella. An umbrella will protect us from the rain. The umbrella serves as a place of refuge for us during the storm.

God promises to protect us in the storms of life. He is our refuge and strength when we face trials and tribulations. But God also provides friends to comfort and protect us during difficult times. Those precious people who are a listening ear when we are distraught, the one who will stay at the hospital with you, the one who is the shoulder to cry on. What a blessing it is to have those types of friends in our lives.

What about you? Are you the type of friend who can be a comfort to someone when they face a storm in their life? When someone you love is walking through a storm, the most Christlike response isn't commentary-it's compassion. Jesus didn't stand at a distance to explain pain. He stepped close. He covered. He stayed. Today, be a safe place for your hurting friend. Be the quiet presence. Be the umbrella of grace and love.

Prayer:

Lord, may we be the kind of friends who extend love and comfort to a hurting friend. We thank you that we can turn to you in times of need, but we are also thankful for those precious friends who help us through the storms of life. Our desire, Lord, is to be the type of friend that You are to us. May we be an umbrella of grace and cover our friends with love.

Journal Page
Use this page for reflection, write down your thoughts and prayers

JOURNAL PAGE
Use this page for reflection, write down your thoughts and prayers

God Makes Us Clean

If we say that we have no sin, we are deceiving ourselves, and the truth is not in us.9 If we confess our sins, He is faithful and righteous to forgive us our sins and to cleanse us from all unrighteousness.

—1 John 1:8-9 (NASB)

I like clean walls. One day, I took on a huge project of stripping wallpaper from my kitchen walls. The plan was to paint the walls after the wallpaper was removed. As I stripped the layers of wallpaper, what was underneath became evident. The wallpaper was covering up old, dirty, and damaged walls. What a disappointment!

This experience got me thinking about sin in our lives. Every person since the dawn of time has blown it and come up short compared to God's perfection. We may have even tried to cover up our sin and not want the truth revealed about our transgression. When we try to cover it up, we just prolong the inevitable; the dirtiness of our sin will eventually be revealed. The longer we hold on to the sin, the more miserable we become. Our spirit can become weighed down by layers and layers of guilt from the sin we are hiding. The good news is that God is waiting with the forgiveness we crave. Just tell God. As the verse above states, if we confess our sin, He is faithful to forgive and to cleanse us of all unrighteousness. Because God loves us, He forgives us, He washes us clean, and gives us a new start. It took a lot of blood, sweat, and tears to restore my dirty, damaged kitchen walls, but when the work was finished, it was so worth it. God's love for us points out our sin so that we can confess the sin and be restored.

Is there sin in your life that needs to be revealed and confessed to your loving Heavenly Father?

PRAYER:

Lord, thank you that we can hold on to the promise that when we confess our sins, You are faithful to forgive. Thank you that through our confession we are made clean and restored. Amen.

Journal Page
Use this page for reflection, write down your thoughts and prayers

Journal Page
Use this page for reflection, write down your thoughts and prayers

Unshakable Faith

Faith is the confidence that what we hope for will actually happen; it gives us assurance about things we can not see.

—Hebrews 11:1 (NLT)

If we walk by sight, we must have all of the facts and see how God's plan for us will unfold before we step out in obedience. Walking by faith requires trust. We trust the Lord and His will for us, even in an unknown situation. God wants us to trust Him, depend on Him, and be assured that His plan is best. Faith is the confidence in the trustworthiness of God. When we face a trial, it's important for us to rest in the Lord and trust Him for the outcome. When we are asked to step out of our comfort zone in ministry, maybe a job change or possibly a big move to another state, we can step out in obedience, trusting God knows what is best for us. The more we obey and trust God, the stronger our faith becomes. God desires for His children to develop a strong faith in Him, one that is unshakable.

A Roman soldier's sandal has a special feature, a long spike at the heel of the shoe. Its purpose was to allow the warrior to plant his feet firmly in the ground when an opponent approached. The soldier could keep his footing even as he faced danger. This can serve as a great example for us as we face decisions, trials, and uncertainty; our faith can ground us, and we can stand firm, trusting the Lord for the unseen outcome. God wants us to depend on Him, trusting Him to direct our steps so we can live out His plan and purpose for us.

As you examine your life, do you find yourself more prone to walk by faith or by sight?

PRAYER:

Lord, whatever it is that we may face, our prayer is that we walk by faith and not by sight. May our knowledge of Your trustworthiness cause us to trust and obey, even when we are uncertain of the outcome. We thank you for loving us and wanting only Your best for us. Amen.

JOURNAL PAGE
Use this page for reflection, write down your thoughts and prayers

JOURNAL PAGE
Use this page for reflection, write down your thoughts and prayers

The Good Shepherd

But he who enters by the door is a shepherd of the sheep.
To him ,the doorkeeper opens ,and the sheep hear his voice,
and he calls his own sheep by name and leads them out.
When he puts forth his own ,he goes ahead of them ,and
the sheep follow him because they know his voice.

—John 10:2-4 (NASB)

Today we don't see many shepherds leading their flock of sheep in the fields, it was common many years ago. However, shepherds still travel today with their flocks across the landscape in Israel. And just like shepherds of old, today's shepherds know their sheep. They know what scares them; they know when just one of the flock wanders off. They guide and protect this precious flock because they are theirs. This is such a loving picture of how Jesus, our Good Shepherd, cares for us and knows us so intimately. There is another aspect of our relationship with the Good Shepherd that is mentioned in the above verse, which is knowing His voice. Shepherds of old would stand at different locations outside the sheep pen, sounding out their own unique calls which their sheep would recognize. As a result, the sheep would gather around the shepherd. These sheep knew the call of their shepherd above all the other calls of the local shepherds. They were familiar with their shepherd's voice. So it is with our Good Shepherd, Jesus Christ; if we know Him, we know His voice. In a time when so many other voices can be pulling us in different directions, such as bosses, peers, influencers, and more, we have to be so in tune with our Lord that we discern His voice over all.

We have to discern His voice in scripture. When we have His word instilled in our hearts, it will guide us, it will lead us, and it will help with decision-making. Oh, the tender love of the Good Shepherd for His own. Just like sheep, we, too, need a shepherd to guide us, protect us, and call out to us in love.

Are you sensitive to the voice of the Good Shepherd? Do you hear His call over all?

PRAYER:

Dearest Good Shepherd, thank you for your tender and caring love for us, Your sheep. May we always hear Your voice over all the other voices in our lives. May we discern Your leading and guidance in our lives as well. Amen.

Journal Page
Use this page for reflection, write down your thoughts and prayers

JOURNAL PAGE
Use this page for reflection, write down your thoughts and prayers

Triumphant Joy

Always be full of joy in the Lord. I say it again—rejoice!
—Philippians 4: 4 (NLT)

If you are like me, you often let your circumstances affect your conduct and disposition. Sometimes when life is running smoothly, I can be one person and a different person when difficulty enters my life. Although trouble has the power to take away our happiness, we don't have to let it rob us of our joy. Circumstances may change, and trouble will come, but for those who have trusted Jesus as their Savior, their relationship with Him will never be altered. And that fact is the foundation for joy in every situation. Our joy should not be dependent on what we go through; it is determined by who loves us! God loves us—deeply—and He expresses that love by giving us His joy. Happiness depends on good circumstances, but joy depends on our relationship with the Lord. If we let ourselves focus on our difficulties and pain rather than on Christ, we will become trapped by our circumstances. If we shift our focus to Christ in ALL circumstances, we can experience triumphant joy.

What evidence is there in your life that you have the joy of Christ? How is it expressed in your disposition during hard times?

PRAYER:

Lord, please ignite in us Your triumphant joy, no matter the circumstances in our lives. Help us to choose to receive and express Your joy in our lives. Even when our circumstances give us no apparent reason to rejoice, may we dig deep into our souls and muster up the courage to rejoice. Amen.

JOURNAL PAGE
Use this page for reflection, write down your thoughts and prayers

JOURNAL PAGE
Use this page for reflection, write down your thoughts and prayers

Recharge

But the Spirit of Him who raised Jesus from the dead dwells in you; He who raised Christ Jesus from the dead will also give life to your mortal bodies through His Spirit who dwells in you.

—Romans 8:11(NASB)

So it's Sunday morning, as you are getting ready to leave for church, and you discover your car has a dead battery! The only way to recharge your battery is to use jumper cables. Your next-door neighbor has been watching all the excitement and comes over with cables to help rescue you. A few minutes later, your battery is charged, and all is well.

Isn't that how it is in our spiritual lives as well- there are just times we need to recharge. We may find ourselves disconnected from the Lord. How do we recharge our spiritual batteries? Plug ourselves back in! Take time to pray, read the Bible, and perhaps listen to worship music. It will help to recharge us. Remember that the same Spirit that raised Jesus from the dead lives in you. Believe and trust that you have power from the Lord today!

Do you need to recharge your spiritual life? Take time to plug yourself back in.

PRAYER:

Lord, there are times in our spiritual lives when we find that we need a recharge. Please help us to reconnect to the power of the Holy Spirit. Maybe we haven't prayed in a while or read Your word, draw us to Yourself, and cause us to reconnect. Amen.

Journal Page
Use this page for reflection, write down your thoughts and prayers

JOURNAL PAGE
Use this page for reflection, write down your thoughts and prayers

Faithful Provider

My God will supply all your needs according to His riches
in glory in Christ Jesus.

—Philippians 4:19 (NASB)

Faithful means to be reliable. We can rely on God to do what He says in His own time and in His way. The above verse states that He will supply all our needs, and we can be sure He will faithfully provide for us as He promises. We may find ourselves in a place where we have to wait on the Lord to provide for a specific need, but it doesn't mean He has forgotten.

Oh my goodness! As I think about God's faithful provision in my life and my family's life, it just fills my heart with gratitude—the times of provision are countless! I do recall a specific time when I was a fairly new Christian, and my church announced to the congregation that we were contributing to a Christmas offering for Foreign Missions. I felt strongly at that time to participate in the offering and to give $50.00. At the time, I was working as a server in a local restaurant and didn't make much. I definitely didn't have an extra $50.00. As the days went on, I prayed about the offering and asked God for help. One night, I went to work, and my manager asked me if I would be available to hand out the Thanksgiving pie orders on Thanksgiving morning, and I said that I would, with the understanding that I was volunteering.

The Sunday after Thanksgiving, it was announced at church that there were only a few weeks left to contribute to the Christmas offering. I felt such conviction to give and believed God would provide. Well, the next week at work, my manager handed me an envelope, and I asked, "What's this?" He said, "It's your check for passing out pies on Thanksgiving." To my surprise and delight, it was a check for $50.00! What an awesome, faithful God!

God demonstrates His faithfulness to us in a multitude of ways and sometimes in an unexpected way, but He will provide for our needs in His timing.

How has God shown His faithfulness to you as a provider? Don't give up hope if you are in a place of waiting; trust Him for His perfect timing.

PRAYER:

Thank you Lord for Your faithfulness in our lives. Thank you for being our provider. Thank you for the comfort it gives us knowing that You are there. Amen.

JOURNAL PAGE
Use this page for reflection, write down your thoughts and prayers

JOURNAL PAGE
Use this page for reflection, write down your thoughts and prayers

In The World, Not Of The World

And do not be conformed to this world, but be transformed by the renewing of your mind, so that you may prove what the will of God is, that which is good and acceptable and perfect.

—Romans 12:2 (NASB)

The Gulf Stream flows in the ocean ,and yet it is not absorbed by it .It maintains its warm temperatures even in the icy waters of the North Atlantic.

Christians are in the world, and yet they must not be absorbed by it. The life of the Christian should look different from the life of those who do not know Jesus as Lord as Savior. The world we all live in has its own politics, financial system, and thought pattern; it seeks to get everyone to conform to its culture and customs. It hates nonconformists—like Christ and His followers.

Christ died to deliver us from this world. However, Christians are sent into the world to testify that its ways are evil and salvation is available to all who put their faith in the Lord Jesus Christ. So, as we separate ourselves from the ways of the world, we seize every opportunity to share our faith with those who do not yet know Christ.

If we, as Christians, are to fulfill our purpose in this world, we must not be chilled by the indifferent, godless society that we live in.

How are you separating yourself from the ways of this world? Does your life look different? If not, why?

PRAYER:

Lord, please give us the strength and courage to not conform to this world. May we stay set apart and seize every opportunity to share our faith with the lost. Amen.

Lord, please give us the strength and courage to not conform to this world. May we stay set apart and seize every opportunity to share our faith with the lost. Amen.

Journal Page
Use this page for reflection, write down your thoughts and prayers

JOURNAL PAGE
Use this page for reflection, write down your thoughts and prayers

God the Healer

He heals the brokenhearted and binds up their wounds.
—Psalm 147:3 (NASB)

When we have an outside wound, like a small scratch or cut, we place a bandage on it until it heals. For inside wounds, like a broken heart, we need Jesus. We need time in prayer and time in His word. In this life, brokenness is inevitable —but it doesn't have to be permanent. Our greatest pain, regret, mistake, or weakness God can use to grow us stronger and accomplish His purposes in our lives, if we let Him. We shouldn't resist how God may be using our brokenness to bring us to a deeper level of relationship with Him. Let go of the regret, the bitterness, the resentment that may fill your heart. As we let go of these things and rest in Him our healing begins and our relationship with Him grows. God is near to the brokenhearted, He promises to heal them and bind up their wounds. What a wonderful promise to hold on to, especially when we find ourselves as one of the broken. We can be assured He will give us all we need to come to a place of wholeness again.

How are you allowing God to work in your brokenness to bring about healing?

PRAYER:

Thank you Lord for the promise of healing us when we find ourselves brokenhearted. We trust You to make us whole again, in Your time and in Your way. Amen.

JOURNAL PAGE
Use this page for reflection, write down your thoughts and prayers

JOURNAL PAGE
Use this page for reflection, write down your thoughts and prayers

Count Your Blessings

Blessed be the God and Father of our Lord Jesus Christ, who has blessed us with every spiritual blessing in the heavenly places in Christ.

—Ephesians 1:3 (NASB)

When we think about counting our blessings, our thoughts usually go to the material and physical benefits like houses, jobs, family, and health. These are all wonderful blessings, and we should appreciate the everyday blessings in our lives, even things like air conditioning or running water, but spiritual blessings may not always come to mind when we think of blessings. Every good thing from God that comes to us in salvation should fill our hearts and minds with gratitude and praise.

The Lord has promised us amazing spiritual blessings as a result of our salvation. Here are just a few:

God promises to love us (John 14:21)
We have peace in Him (John 14:27)
He supplies our needs (Philippians 4:19)
We have been given the privilege of prayer (James 5:16)
We have the Word of God (Isaiah 40:8)
Jesus is preparing a place for us in heaven for all eternity(John 14:2-3)

These are just a few of the many spiritual blessings that we have in Christ. They are so great that only the almighty, sovereign God of the universe could have made them.

What are the typical things that you usually count as your blessings? How often do spiritual blessings come to mind?

PRAYER:

Heavenly Father, thank you for our material and physical blessings in our lives. We especially thank you for our spiritual blessings—may never forget about these amazing promised blessings. Amen.

Journal Page
Use this page for reflection, write down your thoughts and prayers

JOURNAL PAGE
Use this page for reflection, write down your thoughts and prayers

Waiting On The Lord

Wait for the Lord; be strong and let your heart take courage;
yes wait for the Lord.

—Psalm 27:14 (NASB)

In this hurry-up world, having to wait for anything can cause us to lose our temper, our good sense, and our self-control! No one likes waiting. We don't like waiting at a red light. We don't like waiting in line at the grocery store. We don't like waiting for dinner. We want what we want now! So, when we are asked to wait on the Lord, it sends chills up our spine. Why is it so hard for us to wait? We like control, and it is difficult for us to surrender that control. We also like to have what we want on our timetable, not the Lord's.

We may be waiting on a job, or finding a mate, starting a family, or making a move, and God is saying wait on me before you take the next step. It's easier to wait patiently when we understand that God is wiser than we are and blessings follow obedience. So, in the waiting, we trust His timing, and we trust Him for the outcome. It is in God's waiting room that we learn the greatest lessons, and our faith is stretched the most. We are to be strong and take courage and wait on the Lord!

Are you waiting on the Lord today? Don't lose heart, God is working through the waiting.

> ## Prayer:
>
> Lord, forgive our impatience. We know that it is wise to wait on You and trust Your timing, we ask for Your help as we wait. Thank you for loving us unconditionally and wanting what is best for us. Amen.

JOURNAL PAGE
Use this page for reflection, write down your thoughts and prayers

Journal Page
Use this page for reflection, write down your thoughts and prayers

God's Perfect Timing

For everything there is a season; a time for every activity
under heaven.

—Ecclesiastes 3:1 (NLT)

God is sovereign over all things and has an appointed time for everything. If we were to read further in this chapter of Ecclesiastes, we would read there is a time to be born and a time to die, a time to weep and a time to laugh, a time to plant and a time to uproot, and so on. God fixes the time for every happening. This truth became very real to me several years ago. My husband and I spent the day at a local amusement park. It was unusual for us to go without our children, but my husband had won two tickets at work, so we took advantage of this opportunity to spend this time together. When we arrived at the park, I told my husband that I wanted to stay for the evening parade. All day long, I was looking forward to the parade. The time finally arrived for the parade to start, and we were able to get seats on a nearby bench. As the parade started, a lady came by hurriedly, with drinks and food in her hands, and sat down next to me. I offered to help her, and she refused. As she finished her food, I offered her a wipe for her hands, which she accepted, with thanks. She then struck up a conversation with me. I found out she was a Christian, a wife, a mother of four, and she was dying of cancer. We talked, and I prayed with her. As we talked, I caught glimpses from the parade going by. The very parade I was adamant about seeing. As I sat there, I thought well, God had a different plan for my time. We continued to talk with each other and I was thankful God had me there for her at that moment. There would be other parades, but there would never be another opportunity to talk with this precious woman. I share this experience with all of you as a testimony of how God orchestrated this divine appointment. God is working through people and circumstances to bring about His purposes. As the above verse states, "For everything there is a season; a time for every activity under heaven." Be prepared today for a divine appointment!

PRAYER:

Lord, thank you for your perfect timing in our lives. May we be sensitive to Your leading and may we be sensitive to those in need around us. Amen.

Journal Page
Use this page for reflection, write down your thoughts and prayers

JOURNAL PAGE
Use this page for reflection, write down your thoughts and prayers

O' Worship The King

Praise the Lord! Praise the name of the Lord, praise Him O servants of the Lord. You who stand in the house of the Lord, in the courts of the house of our God! Praise the Lord, for the Lord is good.

—Psalm 135:1-3a (NASB)

I live on a lake, and every morning I hear a beautiful choir of birds sing their wake-up song. I believe it is their way of expressing adoration to their Creator. It truly blesses my heart!

What is worship? It is the praise and adoration of God expressed both publicly and privately. We can worship during our intimate time of prayer or publicly while singing during a church service. We can worship in our homes, in our churches, on a walk or in our cars. What is most important about worship is that it is reserved for God alone and it comes from a thankful heart. We have to be mindful of not putting anything or anyone between us and God, this would be considered idolatry, which is a sin. Throughout scripture, we are warned not to have any other god in our lives but the One True God.

One afternoon when my children were small, I noticed them playing in the backyard. As I watched, I realized they were playing church. They were using a turned-over slide for their pulpit, each one had a tie on, there was singing, prayer, and Bible reading. It was the most precious sight for this mom's eyes! As I listened in and heard their prayers and singing, it was so real and uninhibited. It was a reminder to me that my praise should be genuine.

God is worthy to be praised—let's bless His name today.

PRAYER:

Heavenly Father, we offer up our praise and adoration to You alone, for You are worthy to be praised. We come before You with thanksgiving in our hearts for all that You have done for us. Amen.

Journal Page
Use this page for reflection, write down your thoughts and prayers

JOURNAL PAGE
Use this page for reflection, write down your thoughts and prayers

Anticipation

As the deer pants for the water brooks, so my soul pants for You, O God.

—Psalm 42:1 (NASB)

I have witnessed the deer coming to the water during the hot, humid summers in Arkansas. It appears as though they crave the water to quench their thirst. Once they spend some time at the shoreline, they leave satisfied.

What about our relationship with the Lord? Shouldn't we crave time with Him? Crave time in His word? Shouldn't there be an anticipation as we wait for our next intimate moment with our Savior? All questions to ponder as we evaluate our relationship with the Lord.

As I end this devotional, my prayer has been for you, the reader, to have been inspired and encouraged these last forty days. My hope is that the time you have spent in prayer, Bible reading, and journaling has caused a craving in your soul that only Jesus can satisfy.

My precious friend, may our Lord continue to bless you and keep you in His care.

PRAYER:

O' Lord, as the deer longs for the water brook, our souls long for You! Our deepest longing is for only You. We love You. Amen.

JOURNAL PAGE
Use this page for reflection, write down your thoughts and prayers

JOURNAL PAGE
Use this page for reflection, write down your thoughts and prayers